AF593565

Dr. Harvey and the 8 Fallacies of Distributed Computing

Published by:
Particular Software
2 Bnei Brit Street
Haifa, 3475201
Israel

www.particular.net

Written by David Boike
Illustrations by Doreen Reuchsel
Book design and layout by Sergio Cordeiro
Copy editing and proof reading by Amanda Muledy
Typefaces used: Lato and Merriweather

Preface 9

Fallacy #1:
The network is reliable 13

Fallacy #2:
Latency is zero 23

Fallacy #3:
Bandwidth is infinite 33

Fallacy #4:
The network is secure 41

Fallacy #5:
Topology doesn't change 49

Fallacy #6:
There is one administrator 61

Fallacy #7:
Transport cost is zero 73

Fallacy #8:
The network is homogeneous 81

Preface

My path to a career in computer programming began in the same way, I would assume, as it did for many others, creating websites at the dawn of the Internet age, when Netscape Navigator was still a thing, and WYSIWYG HTML editors were not. From those static websites, I began creating primitive web applications in non-templated PHP, with markup and logic all mashed up together, and it was an absolute mess.

But what did I know? I was young, self-taught, and frankly didn't know any better. More importantly the web applications I was creating, if you could call them that, were so simple it didn't matter.

As I grew in my career, my methods improved, and the applications I was building became more and more complex, and soon spilled over the bounds of a single process or a single server.

This is where it starts to get complex.

Like so many others, I ran full force into the Fallacies of Distributed Computing, a set of assumptions generally credited to Peter Deutsch and his colleagues at Sun Microsystems. Nearly everyone (myself included) initially makes these assumptions when attempting to build a distributed application, but ultimately they are proven false in the long run, leading to big trouble down the road.

The original eight fallacies are:

1. The network is reliable
2. Latency is zero
3. Bandwidth is infinite
4. The network is secure
5. Topology doesn't change
6. There is one administrator
7. Transport cost is zero
8. The network is homogeneous

The search for methodologies to overcome these fallacies led me to start using asynchronous messaging, and ultimately to work for Particular Software, the makers of NServiceBus.

So imagine my surprise when I discovered a weathered old journal among a ramshackle collection of old antiques in my grandparents' attic, nearly 200 years old, containing stories and anecdotes that related to the eight fallacies!

The journal appears to have belonged to a Dr. Harvey Fallacious, a 19th-century explorer and researcher, and also my great-great-great-great-great-grandfather. In it, he details his travels and explorations in remote, then-uncharted regions of South America.

I doubt my distant relative Dr. Harvey knew anything about the modern digital age that was to come years after his death or the Fallacies of Distributed Computing that would be officially coined 160 years later. But it does appear that he was definitely on to something, even so long ago.

In this book, we'll explore each of the eight fallacies in detail, including a selection from the journal of Dr. Harvey.

I hope you enjoy it!

Fallacy #1: The network is reliable

On the use of tin can phones in primitive culture

In the spring of that year, my travels brought me upon a previously undiscovered civilization. The people called themselves Ossians, and they lived in an isolated collection of villages in a remote part of South America.

Being remote as they were, their level of technology was understandably primitive. But I was surprised by the locals' recent obsession with new forms of communication. It all started, they told me, when one of them discovered that by attaching a rope between two clay pots and stretching the rope taut, a voice uttered into one side could be heard on the other. (I neglected to tell them that even as a boy I had done this very thing with tin cans.)

At first it was children doing it, but quickly the village elders recognized the advantages that communication over distances could bring, and so they strung ropes all throughout the village. "A clay pot in every home!" became a rallying cry for modernization.

While the clay pot network worked well enough locally, it didn't take long for problems to begin cropping up as they attempted to distribute the network to surrounding villages.

Proper rope tension could not be maintained over long distances, necessitating the placement of repeater stations (simple one-room huts) across the landscape, manned by a human operator who would listen to messages from one pot and relay them down the line toward the receiving end.

This all worked quite well — until a relay operator would miss an incoming message while outside the hut answering a call of nature or until a predator chewed through a transmission rope. Clearly not a perfect system, but improvements are ongoing.

Dr. Harvey Fallacious
November 25, 1834

The network is *not* reliable

Anyone with a cable or DSL modem knows how temperamental network connections can be. The Internet just stops working, and the only way to get it going again is to unplug it for 15 seconds. (Or, put another way, "Have you tried turning it off and on again?"[1])

Thankfully, better solutions exist for professional data centers than consumer-grade modems, but problems can persist.

As a company that does reliable messaging, we've really heard it all. Don't worry, the names will be changed to protect the innocent.

A registered ISP had two routers: a primary and a backup. One day, the primary router malfunctioned. They switched to the backup, only to find that its routing tables had not been updated in a very long time. For many customers, that was the day the Internet died.

In another case, a project used an Oracle database. Everything worked great in the development environment, but in production there was an additional load balancer and firewall. Every once in a while, the load balancer would silently drop TCP connections to the database. These faulty connections continued to sit in a connection pool, so the next time somebody needed a connection, they would get an exception.

---

1 https://www.youtube.com/watch?v=nn2FB1P Mn8

Just recently, on June 12, a single ISP in Asia broke the Internet for a big section of the world[2], creating Internet problems in Europe.

In general, you can't trust any network, no matter how local or global. Hardware, software, and security can all cause issues. This is codified in the 1st fallacy of distributed computing: the network is reliable.

This is especially problematic for HTTP communication or any request/response or remote procedure call (RPC) style of communication.

Consider the following simple web service call:

```
var svc = new MyService();
var result = svc.Process(data);
```

How do you handle an **`HttpTimeoutException`**? This is an exception that's generated on the client side when there's a problem, but you can't know what went wrong because you haven't gotten a response.

Data can get lost when sent over the wire. It's possible that the web service call actually succeeded but the response got lost somewhere on the Internet. If the web service represents

---

2 https://news.ycombinator.com/item?id=9704952

an idempotent[3] operation (a process that can be repeated without any adverse side effects), then it can simply be retried. But what if that process charges a credit card?

Solutions

To provide a truly reliable system, you must accept that cross-network communication will not always be possible. Because we can't guarantee that an attempt at communication will be successful, we need to provide a facility to automatically retry after failures. To protect against failure while in the midst of a retry, we can use a pattern called **store and forward**. Instead of directly sending data to a remote server, we can store it in local storage. This way, when we boot up again, we are ready to continue right where we left off. We can use transactions to ensure that we keep retrying until processing succeeds.

This rises above the level of a simple retry loop around a web service invocation, which would fail if the server it was running on crashed. We need additional infrastructure to make these guarantees.

---

3 https://en.wikipedia.org/wiki/Idempotence

Asynchronous messaging

There are many different technologies out there, called **reliable messaging** or **message queuing** systems, that solve these types of problems. On the Microsoft platform, the best known one is Microsoft Message Queuing (MSMQ)[4], and on Azure, there is Azure Queue Storage[5] and Azure Service Bus[6]. Outside the Microsoft ecosystem, there is RabbitMQ[7], ActiveMQ[8], and ZeroMQ[9]. Basically anything with "MQ" at the end is an indication that the product fits within this family of technologies.

These queuing technologies wrap up something like a web service call into an isolated, discrete unit of work called a message. The message queue employs store and forward to ensure that the message gets to where it needs to go. It can facilitate automatic retry, as message processing can be attempted over and over, even after a system crash. Some even support transactions, so that the message is only fully consumed if the business transaction is successful. This way, a guarantee can be made that each message is successfully processed exactly once.

---

4 http://msdn.microsoft.com/en-us/library/ms711472.aspx

5 http://azure.microsoft.com/en-us/services/storage/queues

6 http://azure.microsoft.com/en-us/services/service-bus

7 http://www.rabbitmq.com

8 http://activemq.apache.org

9 http://zeromq.org

Techniques exist to enable "exactly once" processing in in environments like the cloud, where distributed transactions are not feasible, but that is outside the scope of this text.

Queuing technologies hold an additional advantage over a simple retry loop. For example, if we were attempting to create a customer and received an HTTP timeout, we would have no way of knowing if the server received the data and was simply unable to respond or if, rather, the data never arrived at all.

Retrying brings with it the possibility for server-side duplication. If we retry the attempt to create the customer, we may accidentally create the customer twice.

Message queues bring with them the concept of a message ID so that the server can decide whether an attempt is a retry or not. In essence, messaging allows deduplication on the server side.

Abandon request/response

Asynchronous messaging requires a slight change in thinking because it does not provide the ability to do the traditional request/response seen in typical web service calls.

Sending a message to a message queue is a fire-and-forget operation. You drop a message in a queue, and eventually it makes its way to the server and the server will process it. You do not get an immediate return value on the next line of code.

Ultimately, by solving certain infrastructure issues, asynchronous messaging forces you to redesign the logical flow of your system.

This is the difficult leap of queueing technologies: not that they have an API that is difficult to use (they don't), but that they require letting go of more traditional request/response programming models.

Unfortunately, you can't just take a system using HTTP, plug in a queue, and ship it. It requires a significant redesign, and sometimes rewrite, of your system.

That can be scary, but the results are worth it.

Summary

Compared with a few decades ago, networks are fairly reliable — except for when they're not. As we continue to build larger and more globally distributed systems, we make ourselves susceptible to all the bad things that can happen.

In order to deal with this, we're going to have to move away from synchronous request/response-type programming. The object-oriented model of invoking a method (known as remote procedure call, or RPC) tends to break down to conditions when the network is unreliable, putting our system into a non-deterministic state that is very difficult to get out of.

In the last several decades since the creation of the first computer networks, we have been unable to completely solve the problem of network reliability. It stands to reason that this will not change in the next 5–10 years. We need to learn to build systems that will work in this environment today.

Fallacy #2: Latency is zero

On the efficacy of messages in bottles

Upon the return from my visit with the newly-discovered Ossian society, it happened that my ship capsized and I was marooned for a time on a tiny deserted island somewhere in the Caribbean Sea.

One might think that the biggest problem with being marooned would be finding food for survival, but that was not the case on this island. Coconut and pineapple trees grew all over, and as luck would have it, I stumbled across a hidden cache of rations likely left behind by Spanish explorers or pirates. Among the supplies were dried and preserved meats and a collection of rum in glass bottles.

The biggest problem when stranded, after finding food and shelter, is keeping one's own mind occupied. One day, I took a discarded rum bottle, inserted a note, and threw it into the sea.

Imagine my surprise when, approximately six months later (to my count), I observed the selfsame rum bottle washing to shore. Pulling the stopper out of the bottle, I removed the note and was astonished to find that it was not the one I had originally written!

My excitement waned when I read its contents: "Received your message. Happy to help. Where are you?"

Furious with myself, I wrote another message, describing my island's position in relation to the moon and stars, and returned the bottle once again to the surf. I began drinking rum at a furious pace, emptying bottles so I could send a new message once per week.

Luckily, ocean currents in the region proved to be consistent, for six months later I observed white sails on the horizon. Soon thereafter, my rescuers made landfall. I thanked them profusely but found myself severely irritated that, had I only included my position in my first message, my rescue could have been hastened by six months.

Dr. Harvey Fallacious
August 3, 1835

Latency is *not* zero

The speed of light is actually quite slow. Light emitted from the sun this very instant will not reach us here on Earth for 8.3 minutes. It takes a full 5.5 hours for sunlight to reach Pluto and 4.24 years to reach our closest neighboring star, Proxima Centauri. And we cannot communicate at the speed of light; we must bounce data around between Ethernet switches, slowing things down considerably.

Meanwhile, human expectations of speed are pretty demanding. A 1993 Nielsen usability study[10] found that, for web browsing, a 100 millisecond delay was perceived as reacting instantly, and a one second delay corresponded to uninterrupted flow. Anything more than that is considered a distraction.

What is latency?

Latency is the inherent delay present in any communication, regardless of the size of the transmission. The total time for a communication will be:

```
TotalTime = Latency + (Size / Bandwidth)
```

---

10 http://www.nngroup.com/articles/response-times-3-important-limits

While bandwidth is limited by infrastructure, latency is primarily bounded by geography and the speed of light. Geography we can control. The speed of light we cannot.

This latency occurs in every communication across a network. This includes, of course, users connecting to our web server, but it also governs the communications our web server must make to respond to that request. Web service calls, or even requests to the database, are all affected by latency. Frequently, this means that making many requests for small items can be drastically slower than requesting one item of the combined size.

Ignore at your own risk

Latency is something that should always be considered when developing applications. To neglect it can have disastrous consequences.

One of our developers once worked with a client that was building a system that dealt with car insurance. In the client's specific country, automobile insurance coverage was required by law. The software needed to check if drivers had car insurance already. If they did not, they were automatically dumped into an expensive government-provided insurance pool.

The team decoupled this dependence on an external insurance check by stubbing it behind a web service. During development, this web service simply returned true or false immediately. Unbeknownst to the team, the production system used a dial-up modem to talk to the government system. Clearly, this was not going to work at scale.

This is an extreme example, but it illustrates the point. The time to cross the network in one direction can be small for a LAN, but for a WAN or the Internet, it can be very large — many times slower than in-memory access.

Careful with objects

In earlier days of object-oriented programming, there was a brief period when remote objects were fashionable. In this programming style, a local in-memory reference would be a proxy object for the "real" version on a server somewhere else. This would sometimes mean that accessing a single property on the proxy object would result in a network round trip.

Now, of course, we use data transfer objects (DTOs) that pack all of an object's data into one container, shipping it across the network all at once and thus eliminating multiple round trips associated with remote objects. This way, the latency penalty only has to be paid once, rather than on each property access.

So, it's important to be careful of how your data objects are implemented, especially those generated by O/RM tools. Because of object-oriented abstraction, it's not always easy to know if a property will just access local data already in memory or if it will require a costly network round trip to retrieve. `SELECT N+1` queries[11] are just one specific example of the second fallacy of distributed computing rearing its ugly head.

Solutions

To combat latency, we can first optimize the geography so that the distance to be crossed is as short as possible. Once we have committed to making the round trip and paying the latency penalty, we can optimize to get as much out of it as possible.

Accounting for geography

For minimum latency, communicating servers should be as close together as possible. Shorter overall network round trips with fewer hops will reduce the effect of latency within our applications.

11 http://stackoverflow.com/questions/97197/what-is-the-n1-selects-issue

One strategy specifically for web content involves the use of a content delivery network (CDN)[12] to bring resources closer to the client. This is especially useful with resources that don't often change, such as images, videos, and other high-bandwidth items.

Latency typically isn't much of a problem within an on-premise data center with gigabit Ethernet connections. But when designing for the cloud, special attention should be paid to having our cloud resources deployed to the same availability zone. If we are to fail over to a secondary availability zone, all of the related resources should fail over together so that we do not encounter a situation in which an application server in one zone is forced to communicate with a database in another.

Go big or don't go

After accounting for geography, the best strategy to avoid latency involves optimizing how and when those communications take place.

When you're forced to cross the network, it's advisable to take all the data you might need with you. Clearly this is a double-edged sword because downloading 100 MB of data when you need 5 KB isn't a good solution, either. At the very least, inter-object "chit-chat" should not need to cross the network. Ultimately, though, experience is required to analyze the use for the data. Access to that data can then be optimized to

---

12 https://en.wikipedia.org/wiki/Content_delivery_network

balance the need for small download size and minimal amount of round trips. This is related to the 3rd fallacy, bandwidth is infinite, which will be covered next.

However, a better strategy is to remove the need to cross the network in the first place. The latency delay of a request you don't have to make is zero.

One obvious strategy is to utilize in-memory caching so that the latency cost is paid by the first request. This will be to the benefit of all those that come afterward; they can share the same saved response. But of course, caching isn't always a possibility, and it introduces its own problems. As it has been said, "There are only two hard things in computer science: cache invalidation, naming things, and off-by-one errors." Knowing when to invalidate a cached item, at least without asking the source and negating the benefit of the cache, is a hard thing to do.

Harness the power of events

With asynchronous messaging, you can publish events about information updates immediately, when they happen. Other systems that are interested in this data can then subscribe to receive these events and cache the data locally. This ensures that when the data is needed, it can be provided without requiring a network round trip.

Not every scenario requires this additional complexity, but when used appropriately, it can be very powerful. Instead of having to wait to request updated data, always-up-to-date data can be served instantly.

Summary

We can use a variety of strategies to minimize the number of times we must cross the network. We can carefully architect our system to minimize differences in geography, and we can optimize our network communications so that we return all the information that might be needed, minimizing cross-network chit-chat. This requires experience in carefully analyzing system use patterns in order to optimize how information is delivered between systems.

We can also use a variety of caching strategies, including in-memory cache and content delivery networks, to minimize repeated requests for information. CDNs in particular are useful for moving content "closer" to the end user and minimizing the latency for those specific items.

Publishing events when data changes can be instrumental in managing a distributed infrastructure. Being notified of changes can help disconnected systems remain in sync.

The speed of light may be slow, but it doesn't have to keep you down.

Fallacy #3: Bandwidth is infinite

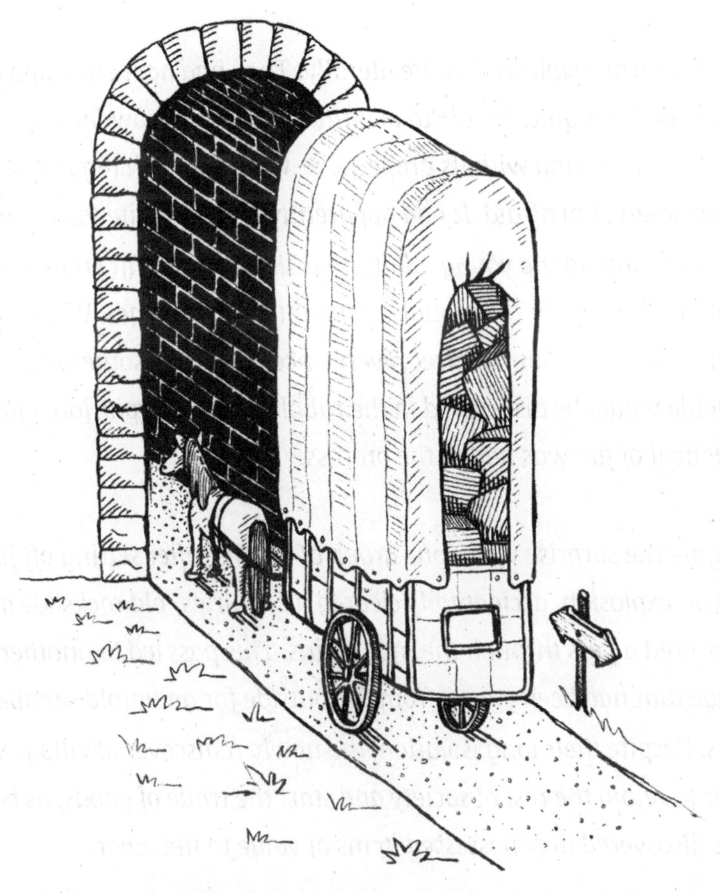

On the quality of trade routes

A few years after my first encounter with the Ossian people, I returned to them and was astounded at the explosive leaps they had made in technological progress during my absence.

I use the term "explosive" quite literally. They had happened upon a substance I was quickly able to identify as black gunpowder and were busy experimenting with its properties—without much regard for proper safety, I'm afraid. It had apparently become quite fashionable, especially among the young adults, to fashion makeshift charges and detonate them up in the mountains near to their villages. While the practice was far from risk-free, every once in a while something valuable would be discovered in the rubble after an explosion. Plus, a great deal of fun was had in the process.

Imagine the surprise when one group of youths, after setting off just such an explosion, accidentally cleared a centuries-old rockslide and discovered a pass through the mountains. This pass led to another village that had been cut off from the outside for an untold number of years. Despite their long isolation, the newly rediscovered village was eager to rejoin the rest of society and start the trade of goods, as both sides discovered they possessed items of value to the other.

The problem quickly became one of geography, as the mountain pass was long and only wide enough for one horse and cart to navigate at a time. At the start of trade, this was not a frequent problem. But as the frequency of trade increased, carts would enter from both ends of the pass, unaware of each other, and get stuck in the middle. One cart would be forced to back its way out of the pass and try again. And as it turns out, horses tend to become quite obnoxious and stubborn when asked to push a cart in reverse.

Dr. Harvey Fallacious
June 10, 1837

Bandwidth is *not* infinite

Everyone who is old enough to remember the sound of connecting to the Internet with a dial-up modem[13] or of AOL announcing that "You've got mail" is acutely aware that there is an upper limit to how fast something can be downloaded, and it never seems to be as fast as we would like it.

The availability of bandwidth increases at a staggering rate, but we're never happy. We now live in an age when it's possible to stream high definition TV, and yet we are not satisfied. We become annoyed when we run a speed test on our broadband provider only to find that, on a good day, we are getting maybe half of the rated download speed we are paying for, and the upload speed is likely much worse. We amaze ourselves by our ability to have a real-time video conversation with someone on the other side of the world, but then react with extreme frustration when the connection quality starts to dip and we must ask "are you there?" to a face that has frozen.

Today, we have DSL and cable modems; tomorrow, fiber may be widespread. But although bandwidth keeps growing, the amount of data and our need for it grows faster. We'll never be satisfied.

---

[13] https://www.youtube.com/watch?v=gsNaR6FRuO0

Problem of scale

The real problem with bandwidth is not one of absolute speed but one of scale. It's not a problem if I want to download a really big movie. The real problem is if *everybody else wants to download really big movies too*.

When transferring lots of data in a given period of time, network congestion can easily occur and affect the absolute speed at which we're able to download. Even within a LAN, network congestion and its effect on bandwidth can have a noticeable impact on the applications we develop. This is especially true since we don't tend to notice these problems during development, when there is very little load and congestion is low.

This problem can commonly surface through the use of O/RM libraries, some of which will have the habit of accidentally fetching too much data. That data must then be transferred across the network, even if only some of it is used. Different tech stacks sometimes exacerbate this problem. In early ASP.NET Web Forms applications, for example, the default method for paging a DataGrid component was to load all of the data, and then accomplish the paging in memory. This held the possibility of loading millions of rows in order to only display ten.

Additionally, we have to be mindful that bandwidth isn't only a concern at the network level. Disks, including those used by our databases, have bandwidth limitations as well. A complex join query may run quickly in development with a limited amount of test data. Run the same join query in a production scenario with millions of rows per table at the same time as dozens of other users, and you've got yourself a problem.

Solutions

In order to combat the 3rd fallacy of distributed computing, there are a few strategies we can use.

"Goldilocks" sizing

The first strategy is to realize that we can't eagerly fetch all the data. We have to impose limits and, to an extent, only download what we need. The big challenge is that we must strike a balance. To prevent running afoul of bandwidth limitations, we cannot download too much. But to prevent running afoul of latency (the 2nd fallacy), we must also be careful not to download too little!

Like Goldilocks (who probably would have made a wonderful systems architect but has a thing or two to learn about trespassing), we must carefully analyze the use cases in our system and make sure that the amount of data we download is not too big or too small but *just right*.

It might even be necessary to have more than one domain model to resolve the forces of bandwidth and latency. One set of objects can be tightly coupled to the structure of individual database tables to be used for updating data, while another set of classes deals with read concerns only, combining data from different tables and transforming it into exactly what is needed for that use case.

Sidestepping

Another thing to keep in mind is that bandwidth limitations and congestion in general will slow down delivery, which we can counteract by moving time-critical data to separate networks.

One strategy is to make use of the claim check pattern[14], in which large payloads are segregated into different channels and then referenced by URI or another identifier. Clients that are interested in the data can then choose to incur the download penalty for the large payload, but other parties can ignore it entirely.

This is especially useful in messaging systems, which work best when messages are small and can be transferred quickly. A good service bus technology will include an implementation of the claim check pattern to make dealing with large payloads more convenient.

---

14 http://www.enterpriseintegrationpatterns.com/StoreInLibrary.html

Summary

Whether designing distributed systems or just watching Netflix, the effect of bandwidth is so pervasive that it's almost like a second currency. No matter how much we have, we'll always want more, and as a valuable commodity, we need to be careful with how we use it.

If we have time-critical data, we may be able to move it to a separate network or cleave off the weight of a large payload using the claim check pattern. Otherwise, we're left with hard choices: balancing the limitation of bandwidth against the limitations imposed by latency. This underscores the need for experience in analyzing these use cases.

We've come a long way since dial-up modems. Yet, the very fact that we still perceive bandwidth as limited today means we'll likely be living with the 3rd fallacy for a long time to come.

Fallacy #4: The network is secure

On the quashing of rebellions

Having grown weary of maintaining a network of primitive "tin can phone" relay stations and frustrated with the incredibly poor call quality, my industrious hosts, the Ossian people, had finally succeeded in training a local species of bird known as "packets" to act as carriers to deliver the messages so crucial to their economy more reliably and over longer distances.

But the Ossians quickly found that this method, too, was not without its problems. The chief of one of the villages, convinced that his village was the most important and should therefore be the capital of the government, set about to use the avian carriers to his advantage. As his village produced most of the birdseed used to feed the flocks of packets, he withheld some of the seed from other villages and used it to lure carriers in-flight. In this way, he was able to intercept all the messages as they traveled through the network and use this knowledge to stage a minor rebellion against the leaders of the government.

The leaders of the rest of the villages, clearly concerned by the treachery of the rebellious chieftain, gathered in the capital village to discuss countermeasures. Many suggested encoding the messages in some way, but no scheme could be agreed upon.

In a stroke of genius, one chief advanced a plan that he humbly described as only "pretty good." The messages would continue to be sent without encoding but would include a small signature that could be used to verify the authenticity of any given message.

The rebel chieftain was finally removed from power when a message was sent by packet containing misinformation and an invalid signature. The rebel chief, not knowing about the signatures or how to verify them, assumed the message to be legitimate. He was led into an ambush and swiftly defeated.

Dr. Harvey Fallacious
July 18, 1837

The network is *not* secure

There are a myriad of security-obsessed organizations scattered throughout the world that take security concerns to the verge of paranoia.

In one such organization I've heard of, there existed two separate networks. Everyone had two computers without external disk drives of any kind. Inserting a USB drive would not work, and trying to use one would instantly alert the sysadmins that a workstation was compromised. To get data from a different network, you needed to browse in a separate room, as workstations did not have access to the Internet.

Once you found the data you needed, you could download it to a floppy disk and then hand the floppy over to a sysop. The sysop would copy the contents to a mirror folder, which would analyze the contents with every virus scanner imaginable before mirroring them to the development network. But that sync only occurred once per hour.

Paranoid? Maybe. If you're just selling widgets on a website, then probably. But if your organization is working on defense contracts or controls critical infrastructure like electrical grids, perhaps the paranoia is justified.

The only truly secure computer is one that is disconnected from any and all networks, turned off, buried in the ground, and encased in concrete. But that computer isn't terribly useful.

Solutions

Unfortunately, security tends to be one of those areas that goes completely overlooked until it's too late.

Check it twice

We have best practices and checklists, but all too often, these go unfollowed. The OSWASP Top 10[15] shows us what some of the most common threats are and how to mitigate them. It's very sad that, in this modern era, the vulnerability at the top of the list is a simple injection attack[16], which is trivially avoided using parameterized database queries.

The bigger problem is that our understanding of the types of threats we are under hasn't evolved very much. By their very nature, our systems are fundamentally exposed, and we start from a position of weakness. Some major attack will hit the news, and then we'll update our best practices to deal with that threat, but it's impossible to be prepared for everything. The attacks will come. It's not a matter of **if** but a matter of **when**, and we simply don't understand the amount of computing power in the hands of attackers.

---

[15] https://www.owasp.org/index.php/Top_10_2013

[16] https://www.owasp.org/index.php/Top_10_2013-A1-Injection

Because of this, the conversation needs to change. We can guarantee that specific security holes will be plugged, but we can't guarantee 100% security.

What have we got to lose?

We need to perform a threat model analysis[17] on our system. What are the possible consequences of a breach? We could be talking about losing competitive advantage, being sued and losing our reputation, having sensitive financial or health data leaked — or we could be talking about hackers seeing our pictures of cats. If someone were to get access to our data, how much would it be worth to them, and how much would the loss mean to us? Based on that, what is their incentive to attempt to hack us? What resources can they marshal to perform that attack? How much will it cost to protect ourselves against it?

After we analyze the threat, we need to bring this to the attention of business stakeholders. Include the public relations department. When the system is breached, who is going to talk to customers? Who is going to talk to the press? What are they going to say? Bring legal in as well to help determine the ramifications of exposure under these circumstances. Perhaps the end-user license agreement (EULA) can be modified to mitigate some damage.

Hopefully, an attack will never happen, but it's good to be prepared.

---

17 https://www.owasp.org/index.php/Application_Threat_Modeling

Attackers won't hesitate to spend thousands of dollars to breach a system if they stand to gain millions. That's just simple economics. But they may not even have to. With LinkedIn, it's easy to find out who your organization's database administrators (DBAs) are. An attack could be as simple as applying social pressure to a DBA to get them to "misplace" a database backup. If that occurred, would you even notice?

Ultimately, ensuring a high level of security is a large cost, and it's all about tradeoffs. We need to have an honest conversation about what those tradeoffs are.

Summary

Security in our software. It's hard, it's expensive, and it's complicated by the fact that attackers are always one step ahead of us. Attacks will occur. Sometimes we will win the day. Sometimes we will not be so lucky. Breaches will happen, despite our best efforts.

While we need to do our best to follow our industry best practices for security, we also need to have conversations with business, public relations, and legal teams so that the risks are well understood and to ensure that a plan is in place if a breach occurs.

Because it's not a matter of **if**, it's a matter of **when**.

Fallacy #5: Topology doesn't change

On the importance of careful aim

The Ossian peoples, whom I was living with and observing, came to the conclusion that swifter methods of communication were necessary when delivery by avian carrier just wasn't fast enough. After observing a group of youths throwing rocks up in the air and trying to catch them in cans (Ossian villages do not boast a plethora of entertainment options), a scientist came up with the idea of affixing messages to sizeable boulders and lofting these through the air with the aid of a massive catapult.

While the wisdom of such an idea may have been dubious at best, still the villagers began erecting giant catapults in every town. Each catapult station, which dwarfed all the surrounding buildings, included a giant metal can to serve as a target for incoming messages from other stations.

Sending a message was a fairly straightforward process. The message payload was placed into the catapult launcher, which was then pointed toward the receiving village, using coordinates stored in the catapult station manager's office. After winding a pulley system, the message could be delivered with the simple pull of a lever, sending the boulder hurtling through the air to be caught in the giant metal can at the receiving side. This turned out to be a boon for the village defense force, as the large weight of the messages and physics itself ensured that their highly-classified communiques could not be intercepted.

Now, as if the great earthquake of 1838 was not damaging enough, the gaffe that followed certainly added insult to injury. Ossian architecture is, by and large, relatively earthquake-proof, but this quake was severe enough to alter the surrounding topography — enough to even cause a nearby river to overflow its banks and change course completely.

The catapult stations failed to take into account the topographical effects of the earthquake and, in transmitting calls for assistance via the catapult system, completely missed the receiving target and flattened a nearby home!

While no one was home at the time and no injuries were reported from this calamity, a lawsuit from the homeowner is still pending with no resolution in sight.

Dr. Harvey Fallacious
February 19, 1838

Topology *changes all the time*

It's easy for something that started out simply to become much more complicated as time wears on. I once had a client who started out with a very noncomplex server infrastructure. The hosting provider had given them ownership of an internal IP subnet, and so they started out with two load-balanced public web servers: X.X.X.100 and X.X.X.101 (Public100 and Public101 for short). They also had a third public web server, Public102, to host an FTP server and a couple random utility applications.

And then, despite the best laid plans, the slow creep of chaos eventually took over.

In an era before virtualized infrastructure made allocating additional server resources much easier, Public102 became somewhat of a "junk drawer" server. Like that drawer in your kitchen that contains the can opener, pot holders and an apple corer, the Public102 server continued to accumulate small, random tasks until it reached a breaking point. Public102 was nearly overloaded, and at the same time, it needed an OS upgrade because Windows 2000 was nearing the end of extended support.

It's easy enough to upgrade load-balanced web servers. You create a new server with the same software and add it to the load balancer. Once it's proven, you can remove the old one and decommission it. It's not so easy with a junk drawer server.

Decommissioning Public102 was an exercise in the mundane, gradually transitioning tiny service after tiny service to new homes over the course of weeks, as the development schedule allowed. It was made even more difficult by the discovery that, because of the public FTP server, several random jobs held configuration values (both hardcoded and in configuration files) that referred to Public102 by a UNC path containing the server's internal IP address.

When finally we had all the processes migrated, we celebrated as we decommissioned Public102. Unfortunately, the network operations had a cruel surprise for us. For a reason I fail to recall now, they needed to change the subnet that all of our servers occupied.

And so we started it all again.

Embrace change

The only constant in the universe is change. This maxim applies just as well to servers and networks as it does to the entirety of existence.

In any *interesting* business environment, we try to think in terms of server and network diagrams that do not change. But eventually, a server will go down and need to be replaced, or a server will move to a different subnet.

Even if server infrastructures are relatively static or changes are planned in advance, we can still get into trouble with changing network topology. Some protocols can run afoul of this changing topology — even something simple, like a wireless client disconnect.

In WCF duplex communication, multiple clients connect to a server. The server creates a client proxy for each instance and holds it in a list. Whenever the server needs to communicate something to the client, it runs through the list of client proxies and sends information to each one.

If one of these clients is on a wireless connection that gets interrupted, the client proxy continues to exist. As activity continues to happen on the server, multiple threads can all become blocked attempting to contact the same client, waiting up to 30 seconds for it to time out.

This creates a miniature denial of service attack. One client can connect to a system, do a little bit of work, shut down unexpectedly, and then cause a 30 second disruption to all other clients.

Cloudy with a chance of containers

With the advent of cloud computing, deployment topologies have become even more subject to constant change. Cloud providers allow us to change server topology on a whim and to provision and deprovision servers as total system load changes.

Software container solutions such as Docker[18], CoreOS[19] and Windows Server Containers[20] allow applications to live within an isolated process not tied to any infrastructure, enabling them to run on any computer, on any infrastructure or in any cloud. This level of freedom enables deployment topology to change with almost reckless abandon.

When taking these technologies into account, it's clear that we must not only accept that network topology might change, but indeed, we need to plan ahead for it. Unless we enable our software infrastructure to adapt to a constantly changing network layout, we won't be able to take advantage of these new technologies and all the benefits they promise.

Solutions

The solution to hardcoded IP addresses is easy: don't do it! And for the sake of this discussion, let's assume that configuration files alone don't solve the problem. An IP address in a config file is still hardcoded; it's just hardcoded in XML instead of code.

---

18 https://www.docker.com

19 https://coreos.com

20 https://msdn.microsoft.com/en-us/virtualization/windowscontainers/containers_welcome

Additionally, we need to think about how changes to topology, even minor changes like the disconnection of a wireless client, can affect the systems we're creating. When topology does change, will your system be able to maintain its response-time requirements?

Ultimately, this comes down to testing. Beyond just checking how your system behaves when everything is working, try turning things off. Make sure the system maintains the same response times. If I change where things are on the network, how quickly will that be discovered?

Some companies, like Netflix, will take this to the extreme. Netflix uses Chaos Monkey[21], a service that randomly terminates production systems so that they can ensure their systems are built to withstand disruptions.

DevOps

Along with the rise of the cloud and containers, we have also seen the rise of DevOps, which is becoming a common part of the software development process at many organizations.

Some of the concepts of DevOps include infrastructure as code and the concept of throwaway infrastructure. With this level of deployment automation, you can recreate your entire infrastructure within minutes, then throw it away and recreate it on a whim.

---

21 https://github.com/Netflix/SimianArmy/wiki/Chaos-Monkey

These approaches, using tools like Chef[22], Puppet[23] and Ansible[24], mean that addresses and ports for locating services become a variable in code that is determined whenever the infrastructure is deployed.

This alone makes a system much more resilient to change.

Service discovery

At their core, service discovery tools map a named service to an IP address and port, something that DNS is unfortunately unequipped to handle[25]. In dynamic environments, especially in the cloud or when using software containers like Docker, a service discovery mechanism allows a client to reliably connect to a service even as that service redeploys to a new physical location.

Zookeeper[26] is an open-source lock service, based on the Paxos consensus algorithm[27], which acts as a consistent and highly available key/value store, suitable for storing

---

22 https://www.chef.io/chef

23 https://puppetlabs.com

24 http://www.ansible.com

25 http://progrium.com/blog/2014/07/29/understanding-modern-service-discovery-with-docker

26 http://zookeeper.apache.org

27 https://en.wikipedia.org/wiki/Paxos_(computer_science)

centralized system configuration and service directory information.

The Paxos consensus algorithm is decidedly non-trivial to implement, so more recently, Raft[28] was published as a simpler alternative. The CoreOS etcd[29] is an example of a Raft implementation, and Consul[30] also builds on these ideas.

It's important to acknowledge how complex it is to properly implement the distributed consensus necessary in order to maintain a highly-available service discovery mechanism. The Paxos algorithm is insanely complex, and even though the Raft algorithm is simpler, it's no walk in the park.

It would be foolish to try implementing a service discovery scheme on your own when good options already exist, unless service discovery is specifically your business domain.

Summary

If you know there will be a potential problem with a technology, test for it in advance and see how it behaves. Even if you don't know there will be a problem, test anyway, early

28 http://raftconsensus.github.io

29 https://github.com/coreos/etcd

30 https://www.consul.io

in your development cycle. Don't wait until your system is in production to blow up.

Even for smaller deployments, it's worth investigating DevOps practices of continuous delivery and infrastructure as code. This level of deployment automation gives you a competitive advantage and increases your overall agility as a software producer. Especially if you want to take advantage of cloud computing or software container technology, deployment automation is a must.

For the most complex and highly dynamic scenarios, service discovery tools can allow a system to keep running even when topology is changing every minute.

A network diagram on paper is a lie waiting to happen. The topology will change, and we need to be prepared for it.

Fallacy #6: There is one administrator

On the dangers of rampaging mules

After a fiasco in which the catapult-and-boulder-powered inter-village communication system mistakenly flattened a home, the Ossians acted quickly to stem off the possibility of any additional legal action.

Although I argued very strongly that lobbing massive stones into populated areas was not good public policy to begin with, it was decided that the program would continue as long as great care was exercised in the calibration and aiming of the giant catapult systems.

Therefore, one and only one catapult operator was selected in each village — a person highly trained in mathematics, physics, and meteorology, at least as the natives understood the subjects. With one certified expert in catapult aim administering the system, it was thought no further calamity could befall the system. Alas, if only that were so.

The catapult administrator in the village where I was staying was quite a nice fellow. I find myself unable to pronounce most Ossian names, let alone spell them, so I refer to him simply as George. One day, as George walked to work, a mule was stung by a bee and driven berserk. In his rampage, he trampled my good friend George. Other villagers eventually caught the crazed mule, and George was rushed off to the hospital.

George will thankfully recover, I am told. But unfortunately, without anyone else able to calibrate and aim the catapult, sending an outgoing message, for the time being, remains an impossibility.

Dr. Harvey Fallacious
March 4, 1838

There is *not* one administrator

In small networks, it is sometimes possible to have one administrator. This is usually the developer who creates and deploys a small project. As a result, this developer has all of the information about this project readily available in his or her head and, if anything goes wrong, will know precisely what to do.

I know quite a few developers and managers that talk about "bus theory" as a way to promote communication of critical knowledge. The central point is this: having only one person holding critical knowledge is dangerous because of what would happen if that person got run over by a bus. The term bus factor[31] was coined to represent the number of people on your team who have to be hit by a bus before the project is in serious trouble.

Nothing so dramatic has to occur to cause serious problems. It's far more likely that, rather than be hit by a bus, these people will simply be promoted or move to a different company. Your organization might be lucky enough to have a person that seems to know everything about everything. You might even be that person. But when that person gets promoted, their replacement probably won't have a clue.

As the size of a project gets bigger and bigger, more and more people will begin touching it. Likewise, as the number of

---

31 https://en.wikipedia.org/wiki/Bus_factor

people increases, the number of communication pathways between those people grows exponentially. On a team of two, the people only need to talk to each other. On a team of eight, there are 28 connections! The chances of all this communication happening effectively (or at all) are small enough that it's virtually impossible the people on this team can all understand everything going on in a large system.

Config soup

Consider, for a moment, all the different possible sources of configuration information for an application:

- Configuration files
- Databases
- Command line switches
- Registry settings
- Environment variables

With a sufficiently large, sufficiently complex, or sufficiently old system, it becomes nearly impossible to know what all the sources of configuration for a given system are, let alone what all the potential configuration values might do.

A trend that complicates matters is the drive to create "mass customizable software" in which every possible option can be tweaked. This drastically increases the number of possible permutations, which makes testing prohibitively difficult. The push for customization also has the interesting effect of creating "campfire stories" around configuration, such as, "Oh sure, we can do that. You just have to enable these two features, disable that other one, make sure these four settings are entered and are integers..."

The larger (or more likely, older) a system is, the less likely you're going to really understand what it does. When that happens, you will be much less likely to remove old code because you won't have any idea if it's necessary or not. This leads to a vicious cycle, in which an already complex system becomes more complex as time marches on.

High availability

The end result is that deployments become increasingly difficult to accomplish without significant downtime. Business expectations regarding uptime are fairly straightforward: clients want the system available 100% of the time! We must then explain to them the concepts of planned and unplanned downtime and how we plan to take the system down in order to upgrade it to the next version.

Of course, we want to be Agile. We want to deploy as often as possible so that we can get valuable feedback from our customers as early in the process as possible. But if a deployment results in five minutes of downtime, we've already almost breached "five nines" (99.999% uptime for a year) on one deployment.

The longer our deployments take, the more pushback we are going to receive from business stakeholders. They will want us to deploy less often, which means that each release will now contain more changes. The more changes there are in a release, the higher the risks and thus the longer the planned downtime. Yet another vicious cycle.

In order to achieve five nines, you need every release to be capable of being completed in significantly less than five minutes. If you add up all the downtime from all of your releases throughout the year, all of those must add up to be much less than five minutes as well.

That's hard.

Solutions

So it's impossible to have only one administrator. Because of all the different ways to configure our applications and their sheer size and scope, eventually we'll get to the point where it's impossible to deploy our applications in a timely fashion so that we don't run afoul of uptime guarantees. It sounds like we're in pretty bad shape here.

Always on

Essentially, five nines of availability means you can never turn the system off. This means you need to be able to upgrade it while it's still running, which in turn means that, to perform updates, you must be able to run multiple versions of the system side by side. New code must be backwards compatible with the previous version, which isn't anything that the administrator can do. That's on developers.

It's hard enough to test one version of software in isolation. How do we test two versions running side by side? When running side-by-side versions, managing configuration — both where the configuration information comes from and how it changes from one version to the next — becomes a big deal.

Even if some magical technology were available that would guarantee our servers would never go down, our upgrades would cause the system to experience down time. The only way to deal with this is to close the loop between developers and administrators. Developers must be as responsible for writing backwards-compatible code as administrators are to deploy it on highly available infrastructure, in such a way that deployments can run side by side.

Decoupling is key

With the addition of asynchronous messaging using queues, always-on availability and side-by-side deployments become much easier to implement. This decouples the sender (generally a website) from the processing of that request. Therefore, even when the back-end service is unavailable, the web server can continue to dump requests into the queue, and the overall system remains available.

This gives our administrators a lot of power. Using queues, we can enable the administrator to take down parts of the system for maintenance without adversely affecting the response time.

Additionally, the use of queues and messages forces work into discrete units, and there's no reason we can't deploy multiple versions of a message handler at the same time, each gathering work from the same queue using the competing consumer pattern[32]. Assuming the vNext version of the handler does not misbehave, we can promote it and decommission the old handler. Or if an error is found, the vNext handler can be removed from service, and the messages it failed to process can be rerouted to the old handler.

This decoupling between sender and receiver also forces us to codify what the exchanged messages look like, and it guides us toward the direction of backward compatibility and facilitates

---

32 http://www.enterpriseintegrationpatterns.com/CompetingConsumers.html

continuous deployment. No longer do we have to bring the entire system down, upgrade, hope for the best, and then restore from backup when things go wrong. Now we can bring down small parts of the system, operating on well-defined message contracts, and we only need to guarantee that a small subset of functionality continues to work as expected after the upgrade is complete.

Everything is logged?

It's also important to consider how to pinpoint problems in deployment scenarios. It's common to take the worldview of "if there's a problem, it will be logged." But how often is an entry in a log file insufficient to determine the true cause of a problem?

Generally, hunting down bugs falls on the shoulders of junior developers. That way, as long as everything is logged, somebody will take care of it (as long as that somebody isn't us). Therefore, we don't feel the pain, and we don't invest our thinking into trying to make it better.

With the addition of messaging, we are given more possibilities for tracking down problems. Rather than dig through log files, we know that a failure occurs because a message fails to be processed and is moved to an error queue for evaluation. Bound up within that message is not only the stack trace but also all of the data that caused that error to occur.

Summary

The ramifications of the 7th fallacy of distributed computing run quite a bit deeper than what might at first be assumed. There is never one administrator. If there were, we would be in trouble when they got promoted. Everyone working on the project is an administrator in some respects. All possess some of the required knowledge, but seldom do they possess all of it.

With all of these different players and the general tendency of software to become more complex over time, we need to take action to ensure we will be able to deploy our software successfully without downtime.

By introducing messaging and carving our monolithic system up into several smaller, independently deployed pieces, we gain two critical abilities. First, we can take down only a small portion of the system for an upgrade, without noticeable effect on the system as a whole. Second, we can deploy different versions of these components side by side in order to verify that they are production-ready without reaching an "upgrade point of no return," beyond which we would be forced to recover from backups.

As an added bonus, developing with this architectural style guides us toward making our upgrades backwards compatible in the first place.

There are many administrators. For all of us, high availability is the primary goal, but it's not something that can be added in afterwards. In order to achieve the goal, we must create an architecture that enables it in the first place.

Fallacy #7: Transport cost is zero

On the care and feeding of packets

After much work on my latest scientific endeavor, a study of the seven-horned elephant frogs of South America, it came time that I needed to send a draft of my research paper back to my colleagues at Oxxford for review.

The Ossians assured me that the best method for transmitting my work back to the university was to use the communication system they had developed that delivered messages attached to the leg of a local species of bird known as "packets." Packets had been trained to be quite reliable and were bred in many different sizes. Surely there was one large and strong enough to fly my manuscript all the way to its destination in England.

Having myself only observed the packet, I found the process of hiring one simply fascinating. Packets, as it turns out, become quite punchy when not fed properly. Due to this and their razor-sharp beaks, their handlers must wear heavy leather gloves to avoid injury.

While packets do not seem to mind how far they are asked to fly, they do require payment for services, after a fashion. Before consenting to carry a message, they must be fed an amount of food proportional to the weight of the message. Then, upon their arrival at their destination, they must be fed the same amount again to deliver the message to its final recipient.

My manuscript, unfortunately, is quite long, and as I have a limited amount of local currency, there is no way I can afford to pay for that much packet food.

Dr. Harvey Fallacious
April 19, 1838

Transport cost is *not* zero

Of course, there are upfront and ongoing costs associated with any computer network. The servers themselves, cabling, network switches, racks, load balancers, firewalls, power equipment, air handling, security, rent/mortgage, not to mention experienced staff to keep it all running smoothly, all come with a cost.

Companies today have, for the most part, accepted this as just another cost of doing business in the modern world.

With cloud-based server resources, this equation changes only slightly. Instead of paying for a lot of these things upfront, we instead lease them from the cloud providers. It may change how a company can represent these costs on a balance sheet, but overall, it's the same concept.

Additionally, we are generally forced to pay for bandwidth. In order to connect our data center to the rest of the world, we must exchange currency for the transport of our bits and bytes. In the cloud, we must pay this also, either directly or baked in to the hourly cost of whatever service we are utilizing.

The hidden cost

However, there's another component to transport cost that doesn't get talked about enough, and that is the cost paid in serialization and deserialization. In order to have distributed systems, it's necessary to take objects in memory, serialize them for transmission on the network, and then deserialize them at the other end.

Ultimately, this manifests itself as CPU time. This usually doesn't get measured by itself. The bigger the packages of data we need to move around, the more time serialization and deserialization takes.

If you're in a cloud environment, you are paying CPU hourly costs, and serialization/deserialization costs directly affect that. Cloud providers have been very successful at marketing their services by saying it's only pennies per hour, which is true. However, there are 730 hours in an average month, and all these pennies tend to add up.

When you introduce elastic scale-out to the equation, it gets worse. Sure, you can scale out to 1000 nodes if need be, but then pennies per hour turn into tens of dollars per hour.

Then the question becomes "how much serialization are we actually doing?" The more that we distribute, the larger the proportion of time we will spend serializing and deserializing data.

Solutions

One great thing about the cloud, from a developer's point of view, is that it gives us monthly feedback into how stupid we were when we designed our software. If we designed an inefficient system, we will pay for it directly in hard currency. In an on-premise system, this would tend to get ignored, but the cloud makes it impossible to ignore.

So how do we optimize for these costs?

Beware premature optimization

We can't neglect to consider the cost of development effort. Trade-offs must be made between infrastructure costs and development costs, both upfront and ongoing. Compared to the cost of a developer's time, infrastructure costs may be too small to merit addressing inefficiencies.

However, this doesn't mean we should design our systems poorly on purpose.

The effect of serialization on performance further strengthens the argument given by the 2nd and 3rd fallacies to avoid incessant chit-chat over the network. We should attempt to keep our payloads as small as possible, being careful to determine exactly how much data we will need to ship across the network.

Right format for the job

We should be mindful of serialization formats as well. In light of the 7th fallacy, bloated serialization formats like the SOAP[33] and WS-*[34] series of specifications seem quite onerous. When possible, consider more compact serialization formats instead.

At a bare minimum, JSON[35] offers output that is well suited for describing data object models and is much more compact than anything based upon XML. It's the nearly-universally-accepted language of REST web services. But even JSON is a bit fat, requiring lots of quotation marks, curly braces, spelled-out constants like true and false — all for the sake of being human-readable and easily parseable. For performance critical applications, consider memory-optimized, lightweight formats like MessagePack[36] or Google's Protocol Buffers[37].

It's important to remember that there is no one perfect serialization format for every situation. At times, it is preferable to have a binary representation of data to optimize for raw speed. Other times, the situation may call for a human-readable format, as making it easy for a developer to

---

33 http://www.w3.org/TR/soap

34 http://www.infoq.com/articles/ws-standards-wcf-bustamante

35 http://json.org

36 http://msgpack.org

37 https://developers.google.com/protocol-buffers

view and comprehend the data may be of more business value than a more opaque format that happens to be faster.

Summary

There are some fixed and ongoing costs in software development that we simply can't do anything about, and that we usually take for granted. However, the cost of serialization and deserialization is something that is under our control. When running in the cloud, we directly pay for it, whether we realize it or not.

By choosing serialization formats that are appropriate to our use case and are as efficient as possible, as well as by being careful about how much data we move around the network at a time, we can ensure that these costs are as low as possible.

And, while one instance of serialization or deserialization is seldom noticeable to the end user in isolation, careful consideration of the 7th fallacy will likely result in systems that, in aggregate, are indeed faster and more responsive for our end users.

Fallacy #8: The network is homogeneous

On the challenges of first contact

By autumn of that year, the ability to better communicate over long distances had made the Ossian mobile hunting parties quite efficient, providing for the society's food needs with much less effort. As a result, the requirement for all youths of a certain age to be conscripted for hunting duties was relaxed, and more and more young adults were choosing to pursue other interests instead.

One such youth I have had the pleasure of getting to know decided to take up the hobbies of exploration and cartography. While on an exploration, he ventured beyond previously unexplored mountains, further than any Ossian had dared. There, he made contact with another people, who called themselves Endians.

Communication between the two societies has proved quite troublesome.

Curiously, native Endian speakers use a communication system based upon their height. As a matter of custom, when speaking to taller individuals (referred to as Big Endians). one must structure a sentence so that the largest words come first. Conversely, when speaking to shorter individuals (referred to as Little Endians), one must begin with the shorter words instead.

To further complicate communication, if one does not observe the proper custom when addressing an Endian, the Endian in question tends to become belligerent to the point of violence. This is bad enough within Endian culture, in which altercations over Endianness are quite common; when dealing with outsiders unfamiliar with their customs, the situation becomes nearly untenable.

While both sides appear to desire peaceful coexistence and mutual trade, communication remains most troublesome, and it remains unclear if the two parties will ever reconcile their differences.

Dr. Harvey Fallacious
October 10, 1838

The network is *not* homogeneous

Interoperability is painful.

Around 2005 or 2006, it wasn't so bad. Most of the code running on the planet, at least the code that mattered, was written in .NET or Java, and interoperability via web services was at least serviceable. Since then, things have gotten gradually worse.

First came Ruby and Ruby on Rails. In the early days, it did not support web services like other platforms did. Next came the dawn of the NoSQL movement, driven at least partially by large companies with no incentive to interoperate. Google built BigTable, Amazon built Dynamo, Facebook built Cassandra, LinkedIn came up with Voldemort. None of these things can talk to each other.

Then came REST, or in other words, "something I invented myself over HTTP." Each RESTful endpoint is that developer's definition of what REST means, which is different from what every other developer thinks REST means.

Competitive pressures, together with companies' desire to create vendor lock-in, suggest that we can expect more divergence to occur in the future.

Semantic interoperability

The true challenge of non-homogenous networks lies in **semantic interoperability**. This simply means two different players truly understanding the meaning of the data that they're passing around.

As an example, let's take nullability. Consider for a moment a software system for a hospital emergency room. Unfortunately, patients sometimes arrive unconscious, unable to provide all of the information we'd like for their patient intake form. Thus, in the hospital ER system, birthdate is a nullable field.

Now consider a software system for a pharmacy. There are many rules that control what patients can have access to different pharmaceuticals. Some of those rules involve the patient's age.

The ER system contains null birthdates, and the pharmacy system requires it. How do we integrate these two systems?

Solutions

Unfortunately, there are no easy solutions for these problems. The good news for us as developers is that it likely will provide us with job security for a long time to come.

The only real recourse we have is to get business stakeholders in a room together with developers to hash out the problem domain. We have to budget and plan for this, and generally, it will take a lot more time than you might think.

First, it can take a long time just to get the right people in the same room and talking to each other. Once you do, you may even find that business stakeholders will start to argue about the problem domain. People from different departments may get into a fight about what the definition of a patient is. How can we design software for something the business can't even agree on?

In any case, this is not an argument you want to happen two weeks before you go live.

Summary

Technologically, we live in a diverse world, and challenges are likely to increase as that diversity increases. Software is eating the world, and somebody has to get all that software to talk to each other.

That's where we come in. There are no easy answers. As developers, it falls upon us to get business stakeholders together as early as possible to hammer out these problems before they become showstoppers.

We just have to work through the problems, using the tool located between our ears as best we can.